To God be all the Glory.

I pray God's blessing upon you as you study the material I have put together. May He open your mind to receive this information and live by it.

Andrew

Verse by Verse Study of the Book of 1 John

Cover Page Design & Photography by

Jess Du Toit Photography

jessejdt@gmail.com

Contents

Introduction to this study

This study comprises questions based on the various verses of Scripture taken from the Book of 1 John. Section 1 highlights verses from the book that draws particular attention to specific principles within the Book of 1 John. Section 2 is the verse-by-verse study that requires the reader to complete the questions and tasks. If this is done in a cell group environment, these answers should be discussed within the group. Within each section, additional study questions are asked that will require independent study. These questions need careful research and answering.

This book serves as a workbook to record the answers to the questions. Additional space may also be required to work through the more extended research questions.

Access to commentary is advisable to answer the questions, although the actual Bible reading and the discussion will result in in-depth, thoughtful answers in many cases.

Answering the questions is not a race. Careful thought should go into writing down the answers, specifically the life application of these questions and their answers.

Engaging in a Bible Study suggests that the reader recognises their need to understand Scripture and the depth of wisdom that follows knowing and understanding God and His ways. This is a spiritual journey and takes time as you investigate the verses, their meaning as the writer intended and their life application. Ensure prayer precedes each step of the way, allowing the Holy Spirit to guide you, opening your heart and mind to the knowledge of God.

This study matters as it might apply to your life's reality. In other words, this study considers the Book's Theology and other principles derived from the book within a framework that makes it easier to apply principles to our daily lives. This study is not a commentary, and although specific information about each book is provided, this study does not engage in textual criticism.

PART 1:

General Information

The Book of 1 John in the Bible

The book of 1 John is located in the New Testament and is found between the Books of 2 Peter and 2 John. It has five chapters.

The writer of the Book of 1 John

1 John does not mention the name of the author. However, from the very beginning, church tradition accepted it as having been written by the Apostle John, one of Jesus' original twelve disciples. He was "the disciple Jesus loved" (John 21:20), and Peter and James enjoyed a special relationship with Jesus.

When the Book of 1 John was Written

1 John is a challenging book to date. John refers to the false teachers departing. If John refers to the scattering of Jews in 1 John 2:19 as a reference to the Jews being scattered after the siege of Jerusalem, then the book can be dated to around 66-70 A.D. Some scholars suggest that the book can be dated between 85 and 97 A.D which coincides with the writing of his Gospel of John and the Book of Revelation (cf. Carson and Moo, An Introduction to the New Testament, pp. 676-77; and Findlay, Fellowship in the Life Eternal, p. 49).

The purpose of writing the Book of 1 John

When John wrote this letter, Christianity had existed for more than a generation. Believers had faced and survived severe persecution. At this time, the church was experiencing declining commitment: Many believers were conforming to the world's standards, not defending Christ, and in the process, they compromised their faith.

John was concerned about the false teaching that permeated the time in which he lived. False teachers promoted Gnosticism, Docetism and Judaism within Christian ranks. Other false teachers promoted their version of whom Christ was, taking away from His deity.

John wanted to confirm that Jesus was God. He uses his experience seeing Jesus and having been in His presence to confirm the truth about who Jesus was. John was there when Jesus walked the earth, taught His truth, saw Him die, and spoke to Him after He had been raised from the dead and at His ascension. John encouraged believers to follow their Christian walk. He intended to demonstrate the difference between light and darkness (truth and error), encouraging the church to nurture a pure love for God and one another.

John wanted people to know that God was not distant and uninterested but chose to dwell among people through His Son, Jesus Christ. He wanted believers to realise that God was very interested in the things of this world. God loves and cares for us with the ultimate demonstration of love with Christ on the Cross of Calvary. He sought to assure believers that they had eternal life and to help them understand that their faith was genuine; as a result, they could enjoy all the benefits of being God's children.

Features of the Book of 1 John

Interestingly, there is no greeting or salutation, as is customary with letters. John starts straight away with the message he wants to convey. Perhaps this is an indication of how important he felt this message was. John wrote with authority about his eyewitness account of Jesus. The Apostle's experience was a robust foundation for a defence of Christ, correcting the false teaching that had permeated the gathering of believers.

At this point, he had not yet been banished to Patmos. He wanted to encourage a new generation of believers about what he saw and heard. The community in Ephesus, where he spent much time, was made up of several house churches with members from varying backgrounds. Some were of Jewish background, some of pagan.

Ephesus was the centre of pagan worship of the goddess Diana, or Artemis. Life in Ephesus was drenched in paganism. Believers living there would need all the encouragement they could get. John tells them of their wonderful God and the fellowship He seeks to have with believers.

Book of 1 John Practically Applied

John wanted believers to have fellowship with God. This is, in essence, what Paul was saying in Philippians 3:7-14 when he confirms that his relationship with God is the most critical aspect of his life. John wanted believers to appreciate the significance of their relationship with God and to see it as something to be cherished and appreciated.

John deals with eternal life in 1 John, just as in his Gospel of John. He wanted believers to believe that Jesus was who He said He was and have eternal life (John 20:31).

But these are written so that you may believe that Jesus is the Messiah, the Son of God, and that by believing you may have life in his name. -- John 20:31 (CSB)

According to 1 John 1:3, John wanted believers to enjoy fellowship with the apostles, God the Father and Jesus Christ. Believers are encouraged to live the fullness of eternal life that we have received from Christ (John 10:10).

A thief comes only to steal and kill and destroy. I have come so that they may have life and have it in abundance. -- John 10:10 (CSB)

1 John, however, focuses on fellowship as the essence of eternal life (cf. John 17:3).

This is eternal life: that they may know you, the only true God, and the one you have sent — Jesus Christ. -- John 17:3 (CSB)

John uses Jesus' Upper Room Discourse (John 14-17) as the foundation for this letter. In the same way, James uses Jesus' Sermon on the Mount (Matthew 5-7) as the foundation for his book and Peter's first letter is grounded on Jesus' Discipleship Discourse found in Matthew 10. John will also ground the Book of Revelation on Jesus' Olivet Discourse (Matthew 24-25). In His Upper Room Discourse, Jesus explained to the apostles what their relationship with God would be like after the Holy Spirit came to indwell them (John 14:16-17). John uses that revelation in his letter of 1 John.

And I will ask the Father, and he will give you another Counselor to be with you forever. He is the Spirit of truth. The world is unable to receive him because it doesn't see him or know him. But you do know him because he remains with you and will be in you. -- John 14:16-17 (CSB)

In order to get his message across, John makes use of various synonyms in 1 John with which to describe the relationship between God and believers. These are "fellowship with God", "knowing God", "abiding in God", and "seeing God". John wants to encourage believers to develop and maintain more intimacy with God. The deeper our intimacy with God, the deeper our fellowship will be. The better we know God and abide in Him, the deeper will be our fellowship with Him (cf. John 14:21-24). The result of a deeper fellowship with God is abundant life.

The one who has my commands and keeps them is the one who loves me. And the one who loves me will be loved by my Father. I also will love him and will reveal myself to him." Judas (not Iscariot) said to him, "Lord, how is it you're going to reveal yourself to us and not to the world?" Jesus answered, "If anyone loves me, he will keep my word. My Father will love him, and we will come to him and make our home with him. The one who doesn't love me will not keep my words. The word that you hear is not mine but is from the Father who sent me. -- John 14:21-24 (CSB)

John emphasises that God has given believers a pattern for their life of fellowship: Jesus Christ. We are to strive to be more Christ-like in the qualities we exhibit. The first quality John talks about is light. Jesus Christ dwelt in the light of God's Holiness (1 John 1:5-6; 2:6). Jesus conformed to the light of God's Will. He showed submissiveness and was sinless, clean and consecrated. John also emphasises love as a quality to emulate in our desire to be more like Christ. Jesus manifested the love of God (1 John 4:10), and so should believers. Everything Jesus said and did was a demonstration of God's love. Jesus was holy and selfless.

John confirms that God has provided a pattern for our lives as believers, and He has provided the power to live according to that pattern. So, in other words, Jesus is an external example for us to follow, and He is an internal power to help us follow the pattern (1 John 5:11-12). In this process, the light allows us to see spiritual things we were blind to before (1 John 2:20), see how we should walk (1 John 2:27) and become sensitive to sin. We develop love, becoming sensitive to those who are not saved, nurturing a desire to pull them into the light (1 John 4:7). As we live in God's light, we share God's life, and so we begin to love as God loves.

When we consider John's words to readers, we can understand two things about our fellowship with God; firstly, we can draw strength from Jesus Christ whilst living in this world and use Christ as a pattern for our lives. In other words, Jesus Christ is the blueprint we should follow, and He will give us the fortitude to follow that blueprint.

In our fellowship with God, we can experience life as God intended us to live our lives; we can develop an attitude that will reflect God's intended intimacy with humanity. The way believers live their lives reflects God to those around them.

However, John encourages believers to firstly be obedient to the light (1 John 1:7), ensuring that we regularly nurture our relationship with God; secondly, actively walk in the light (1 John 1:9) by avoiding the darkness. Similarly, in love, we need to nurture the love we see from God. If we do not act on the prompting of the Holy Spirit, we can become desensitised to God's Love. This infers our setting aside our selfish desires and putting others first. In this, our love will continue to grow. In this way, we also need to ensure we honour the depth of our love as genuine and not merely provide shallow charity. We must adhere to the principle that love does not justify sin.

We should constantly test ourselves as individuals, ensuring we walk in the light through our fellowship with God. Why do we love; because God loved us first or want to be seen as charitable? Do God's principles and character reflect how we live our lives? Could someone see we are Christian by our lifestyle?

The framework of the Book of 1 John

I.   Prologue and declaration   1:1-4

II.   Living in the light of fellowship with God 1:5—2:11

      A.   Fellowship with God   1:5-1:10

      B.   Walking in God's light   1:5—2:2

      C.   Knowing the God of light   2:3-11

III.   Resisting enemies   2:12-27

      A.   Reasons for writing   2:12-14

      B.   A warning about the world   2:15-27

            1.   Overcoming the world   2:15-17

            2.   The last hour   2:18-23

Conclusion

1 John starts with the Apostle John confirming his credentials as having been an eyewitness of the events that unfolded when Christ was on earth (1 John 1:1-4). He teaches that God is light showing how God embodies purity and holiness (1 John 1:5-7), explaining how believers have an opportunity to walk in the light and experience fellowship with God (1 John 1:8-10). If they sin, Christ is their advocate (1 John 2:1,2). Believers are encouraged to be obedient to Christ and to love fellow believers (1 John 2:3-17). John warns believers to be careful of false teachers or antichrists and the Antichrist who will attempt to sway them from the truth (1 John 2:18-29).

John shows God to be love in the way He lives, dies, forgives and blesses (1 John 3:1-4:21). John stresses that God is love, and because of that love, we are called His children, and He wants to be Christ-like. (1 John 3:1,2). Through this truth, we should desire to be close to Him through living for Him (1 John 3:3-6). God's love is reflected in our lives when we do good toward others and reflect God's love toward others (1 John 3:7-14). John encourages believers to be wary of false teachers and to reject their teaching (1 John 4:1-6). Believers must always live in God's love (1 John 4:7-12).

Finally, John shows God to be life (1 John 5:1-12). Believers find God's life in His Son. If we have His Son, we have eternal life.

PART 2:

Verse By Verse Study

SECTION 1:

Give careful thought to these verses below. Write down your thoughts about what the highlighted verses mean to you or how you understand what John is trying to teach you. There may be questions you will need to think about.

But whoever keeps his word, truly in him the love of God is made complete. This is how we know we are in him: The one who says he remains in him should walk just as he walked. -- 1 John 2:5-6 (CSB)

Do not love the world or the things in the world. If anyone loves the world, the love of the Father is not in him. For everything in the world — the lust of the flesh, the lust of the eyes, and the pride in one's possessions — is not from the Father, but is from the world. And the world with its lust is passing away, but the one who does the will of God remains forever. -- 1 John 2:15-17 (CSB)

This is how we will know that we belong to the truth and will reassure our hearts before him whenever our hearts condemn us; for God is greater than our hearts, and he knows all things. -- 1 John 3:19-20 (CSB)

You are from God, little children, and you have conquered them, because the one who is in you is greater than the one who is in the world. -- 1 John 4:4 (CSB)

For this is what love for God is: to keep his commands. And his commands are not a burden, because everyone who has been born of God conquers the world. This is the victory that has conquered the world: our faith. -- 1 John 5:3-4 (CSB)

SECTION 2:

Prayer: Dear Lord. Please help me to continue with this study. Please open my heart and mind to receive your knowledge and apply it in my life.

Chapter 1 (READ 1 John Chapter 1: 1-10)

What was from the beginning, what we have heard, what we have seen with our eyes, what we have observed and have touched with our hands, concerning the word of life — [2] that life was revealed, and we have seen it and we testify and declare to you the eternal life that was with the Father and was revealed to us — [3] what we have seen and heard we also declare to you, so that you may also have fellowship with us; and indeed our fellowship is with the Father and with his Son, Jesus Christ. [4] We are writing these things so that our joy may be complete. [5] This is the message we have heard from him and declare to you: God is light, and there is absolutely no darkness in him. -- 1 John 1:1-5 (CSB)

What does John emphasise in his opening statements?

Why was John able to speak with authority to believers?

What do you think is the foundation of our fellowship with God?

Do you think the unity of believers is essential in our relationship with God?

What role do you think the Holy Spirit plays in our relationship with God?

How does the Scriptural record help us see and understand who Jesus is today?

What does light represent?

What does it mean for believers in our relationship with God to strive to walk in the light?

[6] If we say, "We have fellowship with him," and yet we walk in darkness, we are lying and are not practicing the truth. -- 1 John 1:6 (CSB)

Can one have fellowship with God and still walk in the darkness?

[7] If we walk in the light as he himself is in the light, we have fellowship with one another, and the blood of Jesus his Son cleanses us from all sin. -- 1 John 1:7 (CSB)

How does Jesus' blood cleanse us from all sin?

Can you explain how people were saved in the Old Testament? (You may have to do some research).

What is the result of sin?

What does John say in John 1:29 about what Christ has done for sinners?

[8] If we say, "We have no sin," we are deceiving ourselves, and the truth is not in us. -- 1 John 1:8 (CSB)

Do you think people have a natural tendency not to sin?

[9] If we confess our sins, he is faithful and righteous to forgive us our sins and to cleanse us from all unrighteousness. [10] If we say, "We have not sinned," we make him a liar, and his word is not in us. -- 1 John 1:9-10 (CSB)

Do you think people should confess their sins to God?

Does this confession save them? What is the result?

What do you think confession is supposed to do for believers?

What do you think is the most crucial aspect of true confession?

Why has God forgiven us our sins?

Can you think of three things we confirm when we confess our sins?

Additional Study Question:

Does that mean you are not genuinely saved if you doubt your salvation?

Chapter 2 (READ 1 John Chapter 2: 1-29)

My little children, I am writing you these things so that you may not sin. But if anyone does sin, we have an advocate with the Father — Jesus Christ the righteous one. [2] He himself is the atoning sacrifice for our sins, and not only for ours, but also for those of the whole world. -- 1 John 2:1-2 (CSB)

Why does John call Jesus our advocate?

Who is our accuser?

Who is the judge?

Why do you think John refers to the readers as "little children"?

What does it mean when John calls Jesus our atoning sacrifice?

³ This is how we know that we know him: if we keep his commands. ⁴ The one who says, "I have come to know him," and yet doesn't keep his commands, is a liar, and the truth is not in him. ⁵ But whoever keeps his word, truly in him the love of God is made complete. This is how we know we are in him: ⁶ The one who says he remains in him should walk just as he walked. -- 1 John 2:3-6 (CSB)

How can we be sure we belong to Christ? Name the two ways that John draws our attention to this.

How can we walk today as Christ did?

⁷ Dear friends, I am not writing you a new command but an old command that you have had from the beginning. The old command is the word you have heard. ⁸ Yet I am writing you a new command, which is true in him and in you, because the darkness is passing away and the true light is already shining. -- 1 John 2:7-8 (CSB)

Where in the Old Testament do we find the commandment to love? (Hint: Leviticus 19).

How did Jesus interpret this command? (Hint: John 13).

How does John say love is expressed in the church? (Hint: John 15).

To whom should our love be extended? (Hint: Matthew 5).

[9] The one who says he is in the light but hates his brother or sister is in the darkness until now. [10] The one who loves his brother or sister remains in the light, and there is no cause for stumbling in him. [11] But the one who hates his brother or sister is in the darkness, walks in the darkness, and doesn't know where he's going, because the darkness has blinded his eyes. -- 1 John 2:9-11 (CSB)

Does this mean that you are not a Christian if you dislike someone?

Would you agree that John refers to our attitude in these verses?

Do you think love is a choice or a feeling? Why?

Why do you think John refers to these varying groups of people?

Has your Christian growth reached the maturity level appropriate for your stage in life?

¹⁵ Do not love the world or the things in the world. If anyone loves the world, the love of the Father is not in him. ¹⁶ For everything in the world — the lust of the flesh, the lust of the eyes, and the pride in one's possessions — is not from the Father, but is from the world. -- 1 John 2:15-16 (CSB)

Do you think worldliness is restricted to external behaviour? Why?

What does John say are the three aspects of worldliness that could lead believers astray? Name them and explain them.

Are there similarities between Satan's tempting of Jesus in the wilderness and these three aspects of worldliness? (Hint: Matthew 4:1-11).

Which event in Genesis also incorporated these three aspects of sin? (Hint: Genesis 3).

What attitudes would you use if you were to contrast what God expects with these three aspects of worldliness?

What principles are most important to you?

Do your actions reflect the world's values or God's values?

[17] And the world with its lust is passing away, but the one who does the will of God remains forever. -- 1 John 2:17 (CSB)

On what or whom did John base his conviction in verse 17?

What should our understanding of this world passing away do for our faith?

¹⁸ Children, it is the last hour. And as you have heard that Antichrist is coming, even now many antichrists have come. By this we know that it is the last hour. ¹⁹ They went out from us, but they did not belong to us; for if they had belonged to us, they would have remained with us. However, they went out so that it might be made clear that none of them belongs to us. ²⁰ But you have an anointing from the Holy One, and all of you know the truth. ²¹ I have not written to you because you don't know the truth, but because you do know it, and because no lie comes from the truth. ²² Who is the liar, if not the one who denies that Jesus is the Christ? This one is the Antichrist: the one who denies the Father and the Son. ²³ No one who denies the Son has the Father; he who confesses the Son has the Father as well. -- 1 John 2:18-23 (CSB)

What period is John talking about here?

Who are the antichrists John is referring to?

How does this situation with John's readers compare with those that Jesus taught when He was on the earth? (Hint: Matthew 7:15).

What is your main reason for being a Christian?

How can we withstand the antichrists?

Could one claim faith in God but oppose Christ? Why?

[24] What you have heard from the beginning is to remain in you. If what you have heard from the beginning remains in you, then you will remain in the Son and in the Father. -- 1 John 2:24 (CSB)

What do you think, had these believers heard?

Where do you think they may have heard it?

How can knowledge help us withstand false teaching?

Where can we get such knowledge?

^{25} And this is the promise that he himself made to us: eternal life. ^{26} I have written these things to you concerning those who are trying to deceive you. ^{27} As for you, the anointing you received from him remains in you, and you don't need anyone to teach you. Instead, his anointing teaches you about all things and is true and is not a lie; just as it has taught you, remain in him. -- 1 John 2:25-27 (CSB)

What is the anointing that John speaks about here?

What does this anointing provide for the believer?

What do you think is the essence of a relationship with Christ?

What can the believer rely on from Christ within that relationship?

[28] So now, little children, remain in him so that when he appears we may have confidence and not be ashamed before him at his coming. [29] If you know that he is righteous, you know this as well: Everyone who does what is right has been born of him. -- 1 John 2:28-29 (CSB)

What does John say is proof of being a Christian?

Can our behaviour lead to salvation?

How does this relate to James' words in James 2:14-17?

Additional Study Question:

What are some of the signs of genuine saving faith?

Chapter 3 (READ 1 John Chapter 3: 1-24)

See what great love the Father has given us that we should be called God's children — and we are! The reason the world does not know us is that it didn't know him. -- 1 John 3:1 (CSB)

On what do you think a believer would base their self-worth?

Do we become God's children immediately upon acceptance of Christ?

What should every believer strive to be?

[2] Dear friends, we are God's children now, and what we will be has not yet been revealed. We know that when he appears, we will be like him because we will see him as he is. [3] And everyone who has this hope in him purifies himself just as he is pure. -- 1 John 3:2-3 (CSB)

What should believers be motivated to do when they consider their eternal future?

Read 1 Corinthians 13:12 and Philippians 3:21. How do these verses support John's idea in verse 2?

What does it mean to purify oneself?

Does God purify us? (Hint: 1 Timothy 5:22; James 4:8 and 1 Peter 1:22). Is anything more needed to be done by believers?

⁴ Everyone who commits sin practices lawlessness; and sin is lawlessness. -- 1 John 3:4 (CSB)

Is there a difference between committing a sin and continuing to sin?

Would a person who continues to sin be in opposition to God? Why?

⁵ You know that he was revealed so that he might take away sins, and there is no sin in him. ⁶ Everyone who remains in him does not sin; everyone who sins has not seen him or known him. -- 1 John 3:5-6 (CSB)

How do John's words in verse 5 relate to his words in John 1:29?

How does Peter's words in 1 Peter 1:18-20 support what John says in verse 5?

Explain what John means in verse 6.

[7] Little children, let no one deceive you. The one who does what is right is righteous, just as he is righteous. [8] The one who commits sin is of the devil, for the devil has sinned from the beginning. The Son of God was revealed for this purpose: to destroy the devil's works. [9] Everyone who has been born of God does not sin, because his seed remains in him; he is not able to sin, because he has been born of God. -- 1 John 3:7-9 (CSB)

What do our weaknesses allow the devil to do?

Do you think John here talks about people who sin habitually or people who sin even though they try not to?

What three steps can a believer take to overcome sin? (Hint: He arrived after Jesus ascended; Joseph did this for Potiphar's wife; Hebrews 10:25 says this)

Do you think John is saying that believers do not sin?

How would you explain what a believer does regarding sin?

How does Paul support John's idea? (Hint: Romans 12:2 and Ephesians 4:22-24).

What is the idea of being born again? (Read John 3:1-21)

[10] This is how God's children and the devil's children become obvious. Whoever does not do what is right is not of God, especially the one who does not love his brother or sister. -- 1 John 3:10 (CSB)

How does one identify those that oppose God?

11 For this is the message you have heard from the beginning: We should love one another, 12 unlike Cain, who was of the evil one and murdered his brother. And why did he murder him? Because his deeds were evil, and his brother's were righteous. 13 Do not be surprised, brothers and sisters, if the world hates you. -- 1 John 3:11-13 (CSB)

Why did Cain murder his brother?

Why did God reject Cain's offering?

Why does John say believers should not be surprised if the world hates them?

14 We know that we have passed from death to life because we love our brothers and sisters. The one who does not love remains in death. 15 Everyone who hates his brother or sister is a murderer, and you know that no murderer has eternal life residing in him. -- 1 John 3:14-15 (CSB)

How does what Jesus say support John's idea? (Hint: Matthew 5:21-22).

How can bitterness destroy the believer? (Hebrews 12:15).

¹⁶ This is how we have come to know love: He laid down his life for us. We should also lay down our lives for our brothers and sisters. -- 1 John 3:16 (CSB)

What does what John says in verse 16 tell you about love?

What did Jesus say about our love for others? (Hint: John 15:13).

¹⁷ If anyone has this world's goods and sees a fellow believer in need but withholds compassion from him — how does God's love reside in him? ¹⁸ Little children, let us not love in word or speech, but in action and in truth. -- 1 John 3:17-18 (CSB)

What example does John give us in verse 17 of love?

How does James support John's idea? (Hint: James 2:14-17).

How clearly do your actions say you love others?

Are you as generous as you should be with your money, possessions, and time?

[19] This is how we will know that we belong to the truth and will reassure our hearts before him [20] whenever our hearts condemn us; for God is greater than our hearts, and he knows all things. -- 1 John 3:19-20 (CSB)

How do we escape the worrying allegations of our consciences?

[21] Dear friends, if our hearts don't condemn us, we have confidence before God [22] and receive whatever we ask from him because we keep his commands and do what is pleasing in his sight. -- 1 John 3:21-22 (CSB)

What does John mean when he says we will be given whatever we ask for?

If you are living in God's Will, what are the types of things you will ask for?

^{23} Now this is his command: that we believe in the name of his Son, Jesus Christ, and love one another as he commanded us. -- 1 John 3:23 (CSB)

What does John mean when he wants believers to believe in the name of Jesus Christ?

^{24} The one who keeps his commands remains in him, and he in him. And the way we know that he remains in us is from the Spirit he has given us. -- 1 John 3:24 (CSB)

What does John say about the life of the believer who has the Holy Spirit living in him?

What will our lives tell others about us?

Additional Study Question:

Is sinless perfection possible in this life?

Chapter 4 (READ 1 John Chapter 4: 1-21)

Dear friends, do not believe every spirit, but test the spirits to see if they are from God, because many false prophets have gone out into the world. [2] This is how you know the Spirit of God: Every spirit that confesses that Jesus Christ has come in the flesh is from God, [3] but every spirit that does not confess Jesus is not from God. This is the spirit of the Antichrist, which you have heard is coming; even now it is already in the world. -- 1 John 4:1-3 (CSB)

What does John mean when he says we should not believe every spirit?

What should we do?

How do we do this?

What three things can we consider about teachers to see if they are genuine? (Hint: 1 John 2:19; 1 John 3:23-24; 1 John 4:6).

What do you think is the most critical test of all?

Who is the Antichrist? (Hint: 2 Thessalonians 2:3-12; Revelation 13).

What are people who reject Christ doing concerning the Antichrist?

[4] You are from God, little children, and you have conquered them, because the one who is in you is greater than the one who is in the world. [5] They are from the world. Therefore what they say is from the world, and the world listens to them. -- 1 John 4:4-5 (CSB)

Who is in the believer, and who is the one in the world?

Why can this assure us?

[6] We are from God. Anyone who knows God listens to us; anyone who is not from God does not listen to us. This is how we know the Spirit of truth and the spirit of deception. -- 1 John 4:6 (CSB)

Why are false teachers popular?

What is it that makes people hate the truth?

⁷ Dear friends, let us love one another, because love is from God, and everyone who loves has been born of God and knows God. -- 1 John 4:7 (CSB)

Would you say love is a choice, action, or both? Why?

How does Paul in 1 Corinthians 13:4-7 support John's idea here?

Who is the source of our love?

How did God demonstrate His love for us?

Who gives us the power to love?

How well do you display your love for God in the choices you make and the actions you take?

[8] The one who does not love does not know God, because God is love. -- 1 John 4:8 (CSB)

What would you say, the world's definition of love?

How has this view of love come about?

[9] God's love was revealed among us in this way: God sent his one and only Son into the world so that we might live through him. [10] Love consists in this: not that we loved God, but that he loved us and sent his Son to be the atoning sacrifice for our sins. -- 1 John 4:9-10 (CSB)

What does John mean in verse 9?

Is this "life" available to anyone? (Hint: John 3:16).

What would you say does love explain?

What has Christ allowed us to have? (Hint: 1 Peter 2:24 and Romans 5:18).

[11] Dear friends, if God loved us in this way, we also must love one another. [12] No one has ever seen God. If we love one another, God remains in us and his love is made complete in us. -- 1 John 4:11-12 (CSB)

How can we ever know God if no one has ever seen God? (Hint: John 1:18).

[13] This is how we know that we remain in him and he in us: He has given us of his Spirit. [14] And we have seen and we testify that the Father has sent his Son as the world's Savior. [15] Whoever confesses that Jesus is the Son of God — God remains in him and he in God. [16] And we have come to know and to believe the love that God has for us. -- 1 John 4:13-16 (CSB)

What is God's presence in our life proof of?

What do we learn about love from Romans 5:5, Romans 8:9 and 2 Corinthians 1:22?

What does John reiterate in verse 14?

Explain what you think John means in verse 15.

[17] In this, love is made complete with us so that we may have confidence in the day of judgment, because as he is, so also are we in this world. -- 1 John 4:17 (CSB)

What is the day of judgement?

Do believers have to be afraid of the day of judgement?

What will the day of judgement make an end of?

[18] There is no fear in love; instead, perfect love drives out fear, because fear involves punishment. So the one who fears is not complete in love. -- 1 John 4:18 (CSB)

What does John mean in verse 18? (Hint: Romans 8:38-39)

[19] We love because he first loved us. -- 1 John 4:19 (CSB)

What does John say is the result of God loving us?

[20] If anyone says, "I love God," and yet hates his brother or sister, he is a liar. For the person who does not love his brother or sister whom he has seen cannot love God whom he has not seen. [21] And we have this command from him: The one who loves God must also love his brother and sister. -- 1 John 4:20-21 (CSB)

What would you say is the real test of our love for God?

Additional Study Question:

How can I stop doubting Jesus?

Chapter 5 (READ 1 John Chapter 5: 1-21)

Everyone who believes that Jesus is the Christ has been born of God, and everyone who loves the Father also loves the one born of him. [2] This is how we know that we love God's children: when we love God and obey his commands. -- 1 John 5:1-2 (CSB)

Who chooses our Christian family members?

How well do you treat your fellow family members?

[3] For this is what love for God is: to keep his commands. And his commands are not a burden, [4] because everyone who has been born of God conquers the world. This is the victory that has conquered the world: our faith. -- 1 John 5:3-4 (CSB)

Did Jesus ever say that the Christian walk would be easy? (Hint: John 16:33).

Why would someone think His commands are a burden?

Who would help us carry our burden? (Hint: Matthew 11:28-30)

[5] Who is the one who conquers the world but the one who believes that Jesus is the Son of God? [6] Jesus Christ — he is the one who came by water and blood, not by water only, but by water and by blood. And the Spirit is the one who testifies, because the Spirit is the truth. [7] For there are three that testify: [8] the Spirit, the water, and the blood — and these three are in agreement. [9] If we accept human testimony, God's testimony is greater, because it is God's testimony that he has given about his Son. -- 1 John 5:5-9 (CSB)

Why was it necessary for believers to see Christ as human and God together, from His birth to His death?

The early church had to contend with false teaching circulating. These incorrect views taught that Jesus was "the Christ" between his baptism and his death only. In other words, He was human until he was baptised, and then "the Christ" descended upon Him. This spirit left him before his death on the cross. If Jesus died as fully man, He could not have been able to take the sins of the world on Himself. Christianity would therefore be an empty religion. An act of God was the only way to remove the punishment sinners deserve for sin.

When did God declare Jesus to be His Son? (Hint: Matthew 3:16-17 and Matthew 17:5)

^{10} The one who believes in the Son of God has this testimony within himself. The one who does not believe God has made him a liar, because he has not believed in the testimony God has given about his Son. ^{11} And this is the testimony: God has given us eternal life, and this life is in his Son. ^{12} The one who has the Son has life. The one who does not have the Son of God does not have life. -- 1 John 5:10-12 (CSB)

Explain what you think John means in verse 12

When does our eternal life begin?

In whom do we place our confidence for eternal life?

^{13} I have written these things to you who believe in the name of the Son of God so that you may know that you have eternal life. -- 1 John 5:13 (CSB)

What is the difference between knowing and hoping for eternal life?

Which one of these should the believer exhibit?

Have you honestly committed your life to Him as your Saviour and Lord?

¹⁴ This is the confidence we have before him: If we ask anything according to his will, he hears us. ¹⁵ And if we know that he hears whatever we ask, we know that we have what we have asked of him. -- 1 John 5:14-15 (CSB)

On whose will is the emphasis here?

What does John teach here about prayer?

¹⁶ If anyone sees a fellow believer committing a sin that doesn't lead to death, he should ask, and God will give life to him — to those who commit sin that doesn't lead to death. There is sin that leads to death. I am not saying he should pray about that. ¹⁷ All unrighteousness is sin, and there is sin that doesn't lead to death. -- 1 John 5:16-17 (CSB)

Do you think John is referring to the antichrists here?

In which parts of the New Testament did a sin leading to death? (Hint: 1 Corinthians 11:27-30; Acts 5:1-11).

What does Mark 3:29 say about spiritual death?

What does Hebrews 6:4-6 say about turning against Christ?

Do you think this then means that we can lose our salvation?

[18] We know that everyone who has been born of God does not sin, but the one who is born of God keeps him, and the evil one does not touch him. [19] We know that we are of God, and the whole world is under the sway of the evil one. -- 1 John 5:18-19 (CSB)

What does John teach here about being enslaved to Satan?

Do you think a person can be neutral in their belief?

[20] And we know that the Son of God has come and has given us understanding so that we may know the true one. We are in the true one — that is, in his Son, Jesus Christ. He is the true God and eternal life. [21] Little children, guard yourselves from idols. -- 1 John 5:20-21 (CSB)

Can you name five potential idols in a believer's life?

Explain what you think John means in verse 20.

Additional Study Question:

How can I have an assurance of my salvation?

In Conclusion

Within the book of 1 John, broader themes have been explored.

Sin: Christians sin. When believers sin, forgiveness is needed from God. Jesus Christ's death on the cross of Calvary provides for this forgiveness. When we decide to walk in God's light, we show that our life is undergoing positive change. We cannot escape our sinful nature while we are on earth. We must fight our tendency to sin, but if we do sin, we should also be humble enough to ask for forgiveness.

Love: Jesus Christ has given us the commandment to love those around us by using him as an example. The love we show proves that we have been saved. When we show love, it means we put others before ourselves. This is not limited to making a statement but accompanying those words with actions.

Family: We become children of the living God when we believe in Jesus Christ. Being in this family allows us to love others in our family. Our actions and words directed toward others are a reflection of our relationship with God.

Truth: Even though we may be saved, we should never live a morally questionable life. We should strive to be Christ-like, taking on His character. We do this by acknowledging the truths we learn in Scripture. This allows us to see through false teaching.

Confidence: God ultimately controls everything. When God gives the assurance of eternal life, we can have confidence in His word. Our relationship with God is a seal that brings us into a reconciled relationship with Him and confirms our eternal future in His presence.

Accepting Christ as your Saviour

Now. If you have not already done so, consider your relationship with the Lord Jesus Christ. Have you accepted Him as your Saviour? If not, consider the following aspect of Salvation:

Salvation is available for all!

Salvation is the most profound manifestation of God's love. The Salvation of sinners is not based on God overlooking sin. God saves sinners based on His moral foundation and because of the divine holiness of His character. This is known as Grace. It is based on God, so humankind cannot work for Salvation.

Acceptance of God's Salvation is profound yet simple. It does not matter if one is wealthy, wise, educated or otherwise, nor does age, the colour of one's skin or any other difference matter. No one is turned away.

How do I become a Christian?

First, recognise that I am a sinner (Romans 3:23; 6:23; Ezekiel 18:4; John 5:24).

Secondly, realise that a relationship with Almighty God, who is perfect, while I am not. This realisation requires I rely on the Lord Jesus Christ as my Saviour to make me acceptable in God's eyes (I Corinthians 15:3; 1 Peter 2:24; Isaiah 53:6; John 3:16).

Thirdly, exercising my free will, I accept the Lord Jesus Christ as my Saviour, believing that He died on the Cross of Calvary for me and that through His completed work on that Cross, He has cleansed me of my sin (John 1:12; 3:36; Acts 16:31; 4:12).

The results of the Salvation

My sins are removed from me (John 1:29),

I have eternal life (I John 5:11,12),

I am a new creation in Christ (2 Corinthians 5:17),

The Holy Spirit dwells within me (I Corinthians 6:19),

Moreover, I will never spiritually perish (John 10:28-30).

Accepting Christ as your Saviour is life's most significant decision. This should be the goal of all people, aiming to achieve the point of our existence. I pray for anyone who has heard the Gospel and understood what it means to become a Christian by trusting in the Lord Jesus Christ and being born into God's eternal family (Matthew 11:28; John 1:12; Acts 4:12; 16:31).

Decide to accept Christ as your Saviour.

Finally,

The Grace of the Lord Jesus Christ, and the love of God, and the fellowship of the Holy Spirit be with you all. -- 2 Corinthians 13:13 (CSB)